THINKABOUT

Hot and Cold

THINKABOUT

Hot and Cold

Text: Henry Pluckrose
Photography: Chris Fairclough

Franklin Watts
London/New York/Sydney/Toronto

©1986 Franklin Watts

First published in Great Britain by

Franklin Watts
12a Golden Square
London W1

First published in the USA by

Franklin Watts Inc
387 Park Avenue South
New York 10016

ISBN: UK edition 0 86313 432 7

ISBN: US edition 0–531–10295–5
Library of Congress
Catalog Card No: 87–50228
Editor: Ruth Thomson
Design: Edward Kinsey
Additional Photographs: Zefa
Soames Summerhays/Biofotos

Typesetting: Keyspools Ltd
Printed in Belgium

About this book

This book is designed for use in the home, playgroup, kindergarten and infant school.

Parents can share the book with young children. Its aim is to bring into focus some of the elements of life and living which are all too often taken for granted. To develop fully, all young children need to have their understanding of the world deepened and the language they use to express their ideas extended. This book takes the everyday things of the child's world and explores them, harnessing curiosity and wonder in a purposeful way.

For those working with young children each book is designed to be used both as a picture book, which explores ideas and concepts, and as a starting point to talk and exploration. The pictures have been selected because they are of interest in themselves and also because they include elements which will promote enquiry. Talk can lead to displays of items and pictures collected by children and teacher. Pictures and collages can be made by the children themselves.

Everything in our environment is of interest to the growing child. The purpose of this book is to extend and develop that interest.

Henry Pluckrose.

Our earth is warmed
by the sun.

In summer, the sun
is nearest to us.
Its rays
bring warmth.

Why is this girl
wearing so few clothes?

In winter,
the sun is
farther away.
Its rays bring
less warmth.

Why are these people wearing
such heavy clothes?

What do we mean by hot?
Flames are hot.

Food is hot
when it is taken
out of an oven.

Air from a hairdryer
is hot.

Bathwater is warm.

What does cold mean?

Snow is cold

and so is ice.

Food is cold
when it comes
out of a freezer.

Whoever heard
of hot ice cream!

On a cold day,
hot drinks help
to make us feel warm.

On a hot day,
cold drinks help to keep us cool.

Our bodies make their own heat.

Hold a coin in your hand.
At first it feels cold.
Slowly it becomes warm.
You have heated it.

When it is cold,
we wear warm clothes
to stop our bodies
losing warmth.

The fur on the polar bear
and the fat on the walrus
keep in their body heat –
just like the climber's clothes.

Near the South Pole,
the land is always covered
with ice and snow.
It is so cold, that few animals or birds
can live there.

A desert is so hot,
that few animals or birds
can live in it.

In some parts of the world,
ice never melts.

The sun is very hot.
It is also hot inside the earth –
so hot that even rocks melt.

At work, people use heat
to cut metal

and shape glass.

Heat can be measured
with a thermometer.

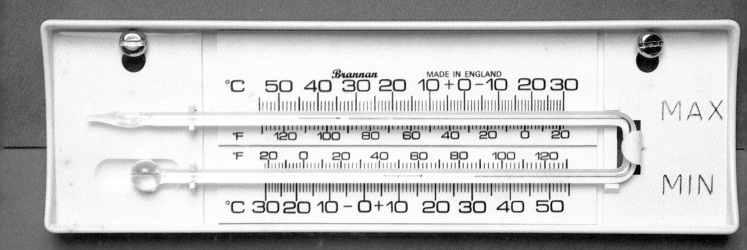

It gives a reading of the temperature –
of hotness and of coldness.

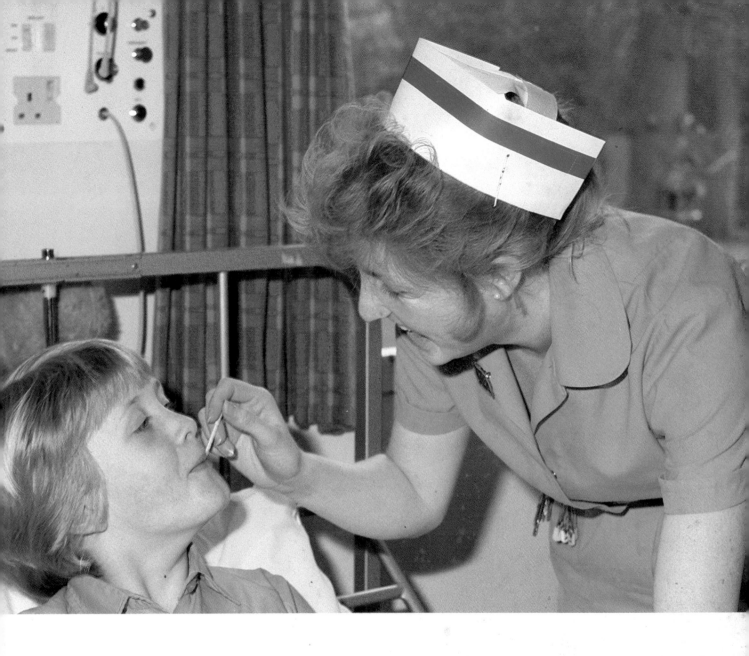

Your body has a temperature.
Can you find out
what it should be?

When the sun sets,
the temperature falls.
Why does this happen?